# Conquer Your Communication

## A Step-by-Step Guide to Building Confidence in Conversations

BY

# ENOCH BROWN

# COPYRIGHT PAGE © 2023 [ENOCH B.]

# TABLE OF CONTENTS

## INTRODUCTION

In the bustling town of Dorset, nestled amidst rolling hills and lush forests, lived a young woman named Lily. While she possessed a brilliant mind and had dreams of achieving great things, there was one aspect of her life that often left her feeling uncertain and anxious - communication. Lily was naturally shy and found herself stumbling over words in conversations, unable to convey her ideas with the eloquence she desired. Her lack of confidence held her back from forging deeper connections with others and pursuing her ambitions.

One day, as Lily wandered through the town's charming marketplace, she stumbled upon a mysterious bookshop tucked away in a quiet corner. Its sign bore the title "Conquer Your Communication: A Step-by-Step Guide to Confidence in Conversations." Intrigued, she stepped inside to find the shopkeeper, an enigmatic woman with kind eyes, who warmly welcomed her. The shop was filled with shelves upon shelves of ancient tomes, each seemingly holding the key to unlocking the power of communication. As Lily read the books, she came across an old leather-bound volume that seemed to emanate a faint glow. Curiosity consumed her as she opened its pages, revealing an array of insightful wisdom on mastering the art of conversation. The book spoke of the magic of words and the transformative power of confident communication. It promised to guide her through a journey of self-discovery and empowerment, unlocking the secrets of connecting with others and expressing herself with clarity and assurance.

Determined to overcome her reservations, Lily decided to embark on this transformative adventure. Each chapter of the book delved into the intricacies of communication, providing practical tips and exercises to build her skills and boost her confidence. From learning the art of active listening to mastering the importance of body language, Lily immersed herself in the teachings, eager to shed her inhibitions and find her voice. As the days turned into weeks, Lily noticed a gradual change within herself. Armed with newfound knowledge and practice, she approached conversations with renewed enthusiasm and assurance. She discovered the beauty of authenticity and vulnerability, realizing that by embracing her true self, she could forge genuine connections with others. The once timid Lily now radiated confidence in her interactions, leaving an unforgettable impression on everyone she met.

Word spread through Dorset of Lily's transformation, and soon, people sought her advice and guidance on navigating their own communication challenges. Inspired to share her journey, Lily organized workshops and gatherings, inviting others to join her in conquering their communication fears.

As she turned the pages of her own life, Lily realized that the journey to confident communication was not just about mastering words, but also about finding the courage to embrace vulnerability and authenticity.

# CHAPTER ONE

## CONFIDENT COMMUNICATION

Confident communication exerts a profound influence on both personal and professional aspects of life, shaping relationships, opportunities, and overall success. In personal life, individuals who show confidence in their interactions tend to foster stronger connections with others. They are better equipped to express themselves authentically, engage in meaningful conversations, and build deeper, more meaningful relationships. Confidence breeds trust, making it easier for people to confide in and rely on individuals who communicate with assurance. Moreover, confident communicators are more adept at navigating conflicts and resolving misunderstandings, leading to healthier and more harmonious personal relationships.

In the realm of professional life, confident communication is a game-changer. It forms the foundation for effective leadership and management, as leaders who communicate with assurance inspire trust and motivate their teams more effectively. Confident communicators are more likely to seize opportunities for career advancement, as they can articulate their ideas, skills, and achievements convincingly to decision-makers.

Additionally, in networking situations and interviews, individuals who exude confidence leave a lasting impression and increase their chances of making valuable connections and landing career-defining opportunities. Employers often seek candidates with strong communication skills, as confident team member's foster better collaboration, clearer instructions, and a more positive work environment.

Confident communication also positively impacts personal growth and self-development. As individuals learn to communicate assertively, they gain a better understanding of their own needs, aspirations, and values. This self-awareness empowers them to set clear goals and assert boundaries, leading to a greater sense of fulfillment and satisfaction. Furthermore, in social settings, confident communicators tend to experience reduced social anxiety, allowing them to participate more actively in group activities, expand their social circles, and enrich their overall life experiences. Ultimately, the ripple effect of confident communication in both personal and professional spheres enhances one's quality of life, opens doors to new opportunities, and fosters a sense of empowerment and self-assurance that resonates in all aspects of daily living.

Identifying the barriers to confidence in conversations is a crucial step toward improving communication skills and building self-assurance.

One of the primary obstacles is the fear of judgment and criticism. Many individuals feel anxious that others may judge their ideas, appearance, or manner of speaking, leading them to second-guess themselves and hesitate during conversations. This fear can be deeply ingrained and often stems from past negative experiences or a lack of self-esteem. By recognizing this fear and understanding its origins, individuals can begin to address it and work on developing a more positive self-perception. Another common barrier to confidence in conversations is the fear of failure or making mistakes. The pressure to be flawless can be paralyzing, causing individuals to avoid engaging in conversations altogether or remaining passive participants. The fear of stumbling over words or saying the wrong thing can hinder one's ability to express themselves authentically. However, it is essential to understand that making mistakes is a natural part of communication and a valuable learning experience. Embracing a growth mindset and acknowledging that imperfection is normal can help individuals overcome this barrier and approach conversations with greater openness and resilience.

## HOW TO OVERCOME SELF-DOUBT

Self-doubt is yet another significant barrier to confident communication. Individuals may doubt their knowledge, expertise, or the relevance of their contributions to a conversation. This lack of self-assurance can lead to self-censorship or a reluctance to share ideas, even when they may be valuable to the discussion. Overcoming self-doubt involves recognizing one's strengths, acknowledging personal achievements, and building self-belief through continuous learning and practice. Developing a sense of competence and trust in one's abilities empowers individuals to engage more confidently in conversations.

## STEPS IN EMBRACING SELF-AWARENESS AND SELF-ACCEPTANCE

Embracing self-awareness and self-acceptance is a transformative journey that lays the foundation for personal growth and emotional well-being. Self-awareness involves developing a deep understanding of one's thoughts, feelings, beliefs, strengths, weaknesses, and patterns of behavior. It requires being honest with oneself and actively observing the inner workings of the mind without judgment. By cultivating self-awareness, individuals gain insights into their motivations and reactions, which allows them to make conscious choices and respond to situations more effectively. Understanding oneself on a deeper level fosters a sense of authenticity and empowers individuals to communicate more genuinely in their interactions with others.

Equally important is self-acceptance, which involves embracing one's imperfections, vulnerabilities, and unique qualities with compassion and without self-criticism. Often, individuals struggle with self-acceptance due to societal expectations, comparison with others, or internalized beliefs about not being good enough. However, self-acceptance is a liberating practice that opens the door to self-compassion and a positive self-image. It allows individuals to acknowledge their flaws and mistakes while recognizing their inherent worth and potential for growth. With self-acceptance, individuals can let go of the need for external validation and develop a stronger sense of self-confidence, leading to more authentic and fulfilling communication with others.

Embracing self-awareness and self-acceptance involves developing a non-judgmental and kind attitude toward oneself. It requires being patient and gentle during the process of self-discovery and understanding that growth is an ongoing journey. Practicing mindfulness and self-reflection techniques can be instrumental in building self-awareness. Journaling, meditation, or seeking professional guidance through therapy or coaching are some effective methods to enhance self-awareness and foster a deeper connection with one's thoughts and emotions. Similarly, self-acceptance can be nurtured through positive affirmations, challenging negative self-talk, and surrounding oneself with supportive and affirming individuals.

Ultimately, embracing self-awareness and self-acceptance is not about achieving perfection but rather about embracing one's humanity with all its strengths and weaknesses. It is about acknowledging that everyone has areas for growth and that imperfection is a natural aspect of being human. Through this process, individuals can cultivate a sense of inner peace and confidence, which translates into more authentic and meaningful communication with others. Embracing self-awareness and self-acceptance paves the way for greater empathy, understanding, and connection with those around us, fostering healthier and more fulfilling relationships in both personal and professional spheres.

# CHAPTER TWO

## HOW TO CULTIVATING A POSITIVE MINDSET

Cultivating a positive mindset is a powerful strategy for achieving confident communication. A positive mindset involves adopting an optimistic and constructive outlook on oneself, others, and the world. When individuals approach conversations with positivity, they are more likely to embrace challenges as opportunities for growth, view mistakes as learning experiences, and maintain a sense of resilience in the face of setbacks. This mindset empowers individuals to face communication situations with confidence and a belief in their abilities, leading to greater self-assurance and assertiveness in expressing their thoughts and ideas.

An essential aspect of cultivating a positive mindset for confident communication is practicing self-affirmations. By regularly affirming one's strengths, abilities, and self-worth, individuals reinforce positive beliefs about themselves, enhancing their self-esteem and reducing self-doubt. Positive affirmations can be particularly beneficial before challenging communication scenarios, as they help individuals shift their focus from potential negative outcomes to their capabilities and potential for success.

Furthermore, focusing on positive outcomes and envisioning successful communication experiences can bolster confidence. Visualization techniques involve mentally rehearsing conversations, imagining them going smoothly and achieving the desired results. This practice helps build a sense of familiarity and ease, reducing anxiety and increasing one's readiness to engage confidently in real-life communication situations.

Gratitude is also a fundamental aspect of cultivating a positive mindset. Expressing gratitude for the opportunity to communicate, the knowledge gained from others, and the shared experiences in conversations can foster a sense of connection and appreciation. Gratitude encourages individuals to approach interactions with an open heart and a willingness to listen and learn from others, which contributes to more engaging and meaningful conversations.

## STEPS IN OVERCOMING SELF-DOUBT AND NERVOUSNESS

Overcoming self-doubt and nervousness is a crucial step toward building confidence in communication and various aspects of life. Self-doubt is the nagging inner voice that questions our abilities and worth, while nervousness manifests as anxious feelings before or during social interactions. To conquer these obstacles, one must first recognize that everyone experiences self-doubt and nervousness to some extent, and it is a normal human reaction to new or challenging situations. Accepting this fact allows individuals to approach their insecurities with compassion and understanding, rather than harsh self-criticism.

One effective strategy for overcoming self-doubt is to challenge negative thought patterns. By identifying and reframing self-limiting beliefs, individuals can replace destructive thoughts with more empowering ones. Engaging in positive self-talk, acknowledging past achievements, and focusing on strengths rather than weaknesses can help shift the mindset from doubt to self-assurance. Additionally, seeking support from friends, mentors, or counselors can provide valuable perspectives and encouragement, reinforcing the belief in one's capabilities.

Addressing nervousness involves adopting relaxation techniques and practicing mindfulness. Deep breathing exercises, meditation, or progressive muscle relaxation can help calm the mind and body before engaging in challenging conversations or situations. Engaging in regular practice, such as role-playing conversations or rehearsing presentations, can desensitize the nervousness and improve performance. Gradual exposure to anxiety-provoking situations also helps build resilience, as each successful experience serves as evidence of one's capacity to handle nervousness effectively.

Moreover, it is essential to recognize that perfection is not the goal; rather, it is about progress and growth. Accepting that occasional nervousness is natural and even acceptable allows individuals to let go of the pressure to be flawless. Embracing the learning process and viewing mistakes as opportunities for growth can help reframe nervousness as a valuable experience rather than a hindrance. Celebrating small victories and acknowledging personal growth throughout the journey further reinforces the confidence in one's ability to overcome self-doubt and nervousness. Ultimately, by cultivating a supportive and compassionate mindset, implementing relaxation techniques, and embracing imperfection, individuals can gradually conquer self-doubt and nervousness, paving the way for a more confident and fulfilling life.

## IMPORTANCE OF BODY LANGUAGES IN COMMUNICATION

### BODY LANGUAGES ROLE

Body language plays a pivotal role in conveying confidence and leaving a lasting impression on others. It is a powerful non-verbal communication tool that often speaks louder than words. When individuals exhibit confident body language, they project an aura of self-assuredness and credibility, which can significantly impact how they are perceived in various social and professional settings. A strong, upright posture is a fundamental aspect of confident body language. Standing tall with shoulders back not only reflects confidence but also communicates an open and approachable demeanor, inviting positive interactions with others.

## EYE CONTACT

Eye contact is another crucial component of confident body language. Maintaining steady and appropriate eye contact during conversations demonstrates attentiveness and sincerity. It establishes a sense of connection and trust with the other person, making them feel valued and respected. On the contrary, avoiding eye contact may convey insecurity or lack of confidence, leading to potential misunderstandings or skepticism about one's intentions.

## POSTURE

Posture is a crucial element of confident body language. A strong and upright posture exudes self-assurance and communicates a sense of presence and authority. To enhance posture, individuals should practice standing tall with shoulders back and their body weight evenly distributed. Avoiding slouching or crossing arms can also make a significant difference in how one is perceived. By paying attention to their posture, individuals not only appear more confident but also feel more self-assured, positively impacting their overall demeanor.

## GESTURE

Gestures are another powerful tool in non-verbal communication. Purposeful and controlled gestures can emphasize points and add emphasis to verbal messages.

Practicing appropriate hand movements while speaking helps to convey confidence and conviction in one's words. However, it is essential to avoid excessive or distracting gestures, as they may convey nervousness or distract from the message. By refining gestures to be deliberate and aligned with the spoken words, individuals can enhance their communication effectiveness and reinforce their confidence in their expressions.

In addition to enhancing each element individually, it is essential to ensure they work harmoniously together. Consistency between eye contact, posture, and gestures creates a congruent and confident impression. When engaging in conversations, individuals should focus on maintaining eye contact, using appropriate gestures to support their speech, and exhibiting an open and strong posture. This cohesive approach to non-verbal communication helps to convey authenticity and reinforces the message being delivered, further solidifying the perception of confidence in interactions.

# CHAPTER THREE

## ACTIVE LISTENING

Active listening is a powerful and essential skill that serves as the key to meaningful conversations. When individuals engage in active listening, they demonstrate a genuine interest in understanding the speaker's message, feelings, and underlying thoughts. The process involves giving full attention to the speaker, maintaining eye contact, and providing verbal and non-verbal feedback to show understanding and empathy. By actively listening, individuals create an environment of trust and respect, fostering a deeper connection with the speaker and enhancing the overall quality of the conversation.

## BENEFITS OF ACTIVE LISTENING

One of the primary benefits of active listening is that it allows individuals to gain valuable insights into the speaker's perspective and emotions. By truly understanding the speaker's viewpoint, individuals can respond more effectively, make informed decisions, and avoid misunderstandings. Active listening also facilitates open and honest communication, as speakers feel more comfortable expressing their thoughts and emotions when they know they are being heard and valued.

Furthermore, active listening promotes empathy and compassion. By focusing on the speaker's words and feelings, individuals can put themselves in the speaker's shoes, appreciating their experiences and emotions. This empathetic connection creates a deeper level of understanding and establishes a sense of genuine care and concern in the conversation.

In addition, active listening builds stronger relationships. When individuals feel heard and understood, they are more likely to trust and confide in those who actively listen. As a result, active listening fosters meaningful and lasting connections, whether in personal relationships, professional settings, or community interactions.

## EMPATHETIC LISTENING

Empathetic listening is a profound form of active listening that involves not only understanding the words spoken by the speaker but also trying to comprehend their emotions, perspectives, and underlying needs. When individuals engage in empathetic listening, they convey genuine interest and concern for the speaker's experiences and feelings. By offering this level of empathy, individuals can build strong connections and foster deeper relationships with others.

One of the primary impacts of empathetic listening on building connections is the establishment of trust and rapport. When individuals feel heard and understood, they are more likely to open up and share their thoughts and emotions freely. Empathetic listening creates a safe and non-judgmental space, which encourages open communication and promotes authentic exchanges. This heightened sense of trust strengthens the bond between the listener and the speaker, laying the foundation for a more meaningful and lasting connection.

Moreover, empathetic listening fosters mutual understanding and empathy in relationships. By taking the time to understand another person's experiences and emotions, individuals can develop a greater appreciation for the complexities of the speaker's life. This mutual understanding cultivates empathy, allowing both parties to connect on a deeper level and see the world from each other's perspectives. In turn, this empathy can lead to increased compassion, support, and cooperation in the relationship.``

Additionally, empathetic listening helps resolve conflicts and misunderstandings. When individuals feel that their concerns and emotions are genuinely heard and acknowledged, they are more willing to engage in constructive dialogue to address conflicts. Empathetic listening encourages problem-solving and collaborative communication, allowing individuals to work together to find solutions and common ground. This conflict resolution through empathetic listening contributes to stronger connections and more harmonious relationships.

## IMPACTS OF EMPATHETIC LISTENING

Empathetic listening is a profound form of active listening that involves not only understanding the words spoken by the speaker but also trying to comprehend their emotions, perspectives, and underlying needs. When individuals engage in empathetic listening, they convey genuine interest and concern for the speaker's experiences and feelings. By offering this level of empathy, individuals can build strong connections and foster deeper relationships with others.

One of the primary impacts of empathetic listening on building connections is the establishment of trust and rapport. When individuals feel heard and understood, they are more likely to open up and share their thoughts and emotions freely. Empathetic listening creates a safe and non-judgmental space, which encourages open communication and promotes authentic exchanges. This heightened sense of trust strengthens the bond between the listener and the speaker, laying the foundation for a more meaningful and lasting connection.

Moreover, empathetic listening fosters mutual understanding and empathy in relationships. By taking the time to understand another person's experiences and emotions, individuals can develop a greater appreciation for the complexities of the speaker's life. This mutual understanding cultivates empathy, allowing both parties to connect on a deeper level and see the world from each other's perspectives. In turn, this empathy can lead to increased compassion, support, and cooperation in the relationship.

Additionally, empathetic listening helps resolve conflicts and misunderstandings. When individuals feel that their concerns and emotions are genuinely heard and acknowledged, they are more willing to engage in constructive dialogue to address conflicts. Empathetic listening encourages problem-solving and collaborative communication, allowing individuals to work together to find solutions and common ground. This conflict resolution through empathetic listening contributes to stronger connections and more harmonious relationships.

Dealing with distractions

In today's fast-paced and technology-driven world, distractions are ubiquitous and can hinder productivity and focus. Employing effective strategies for overcoming distractions is crucial for maintaining concentration and achieving optimal performance. One essential strategy is creating a conducive environment for focused work. Minimize potential distractions by designating a quiet and clutter-free workspace, away from noise and interruptions. Additionally, establish clear boundaries with family members or colleagues during focused work hours, ensuring they understand when you need uninterrupted time. Utilizing tools like noise-cancelling headphones or ambient music can also help create a more focused atmosphere.

Another valuable strategy is practicing mindfulness and incorporating regular breaks into your work routine. Engaging in mindfulness exercises, such as meditation or deep breathing, helps cultivate mental clarity and resilience against distractions. Taking short breaks during work sessions allows your brain to recharge, reducing the risk of mental fatigue and improving overall focus. These breaks can be as simple as stretching, going for a short walk, or taking a moment to enjoy a healthy snack. By balancing focused work with mindful breaks, you can enhance your ability to sustain attention and concentration.

Moreover, setting specific goals and prioritizing tasks can sharpen your focus and increase productivity. Breaking down larger projects into smaller, manageable tasks helps you stay organized and prevents feelings of overwhelm. Prioritize your tasks based on urgency and importance, tackling high-priority items first. This approach ensures that your focus remains directed on essential tasks and minimizes distractions from less crucial activities.

In addition to these strategies, fostering discipline and self-awareness is vital for improving focus. Acknowledge your personal weaknesses when it comes to distractions, such as checking social media frequently or getting sidetracked by irrelevant tasks. Implement techniques like time-blocking, where you allocate specific time slots for focused work and intentionally avoid distractions during those periods. By understanding your distractions and actively taking steps to overcome them, you can build discipline and create a more focused and productive work routine.

# CHAPTER FOUR

## SPEAKING WITH CLARITY AND ASSERTIVENESS

Speaking with clarity and assertiveness is a vital communication skill that enables individuals to express their ideas, opinions, and needs effectively while commanding attention and respect from their audience. Clarity in speech involves articulating thoughts in a concise and easily understandable manner. It requires organizing ideas logically and using simple language to avoid confusion. By speaking clearly, individuals can convey their message with precision, making it easier for others to comprehend and engage with the content.

Assertiveness, on the other hand, involves expressing one's thoughts and opinions confidently and firmly without being aggressive or disrespectful. An assertive speaker knows how to assert their needs and boundaries while considering the perspectives of others. This communication style promotes healthy and open discussions, where individuals feel valued and respected, fostering a conducive environment for collaboration and problem-solving. When individuals combine clarity and assertiveness, they project confidence and credibility in their communication. A clear and assertive speaker inspires trust and inspires others to listen attentively. This style of communication is particularly effective in professional settings, such as negotiations, presentations, and team meetings, where a strong and persuasive voice can make a significant impact.

Moreover, speaking with clarity and assertiveness enhances active listening in others. When individuals communicate their ideas clearly and assertively, it allows listeners to focus on the content rather than trying to decipher ambiguous or uncertain messages. This level of engagement leads to more productive discussions and encourages active participation from the audience. To improve clarity and assertiveness in speech, individuals can practice self-awareness and develop confidence in expressing their ideas. They can use techniques such as structuring their thoughts beforehand, maintaining good posture and eye contact, and using assertive language, such as "I" statements, to convey their thoughts with conviction.

Utilizing powerful vocabulary and persuasive language

Utilizing powerful vocabulary and persuasive language is a compelling communication technique that can captivate audiences and effectively convey ideas and arguments. Powerful vocabulary involves using strong and impactful words that evoke emotions and create vivid mental images. By choosing precise and evocative language, speakers can leave a lasting impression on their listeners and make their messages more memorable and engaging.

Persuasive language, on the other hand, aims to influence the beliefs, attitudes, and behaviors of the audience. It involves using rhetorical devices, such as analogies, metaphors, and persuasive appeals, to persuade the listeners to adopt a particular viewpoint or take a specific action. Persuasive language is commonly used in public speaking, advertising, and marketing to convince people to support a cause, purchase a product, or change their behavior.

When combined, powerful vocabulary and persuasive language can have a profound impact on communication effectiveness. By incorporating strong and emotive words, speakers can elicit emotions and create a sense of urgency or excitement around their message. Additionally, persuasive language techniques can help build a compelling argument, appealing to the audience's logic, emotions, and sense of credibility.

Furthermore, using powerful vocabulary and persuasive language can enhance a speaker's credibility and authority. Well-chosen words demonstrate a command of the subject matter and reflect the speaker's intelligence and confidence. Persuasive language, when employed skillfully, can make the audience view the speaker as knowledgeable and trustworthy, increasing the likelihood of gaining their support or agreement.

To utilize powerful vocabulary and persuasive language effectively, speakers should tailor their message to their audience. Understanding the needs, interests, and values of the listeners allows speakers to craft messages that resonate with their specific concerns and aspirations. Additionally, speakers should strike a balance between passion and reason, using emotion to connect with the audience while supporting their arguments with credible evidence and logical reasoning.

## STEPS IN HANDLING DIFFICULT CONVERSATIONS

Handling difficult conversations with tact and confidence is an essential interpersonal skill that allows individuals to navigate sensitive topics or conflicts while maintaining a positive and constructive dialogue. Tactful communication involves being sensitive to the feelings and perspectives of others and choosing words carefully to avoid causing unnecessary offense or harm. When facing challenging conversations, maintaining confidence in communication ensures that the message is delivered assertively and with clarity.

One fundamental aspect of handling difficult conversations with tact and confidence is active listening. Empathetic listening demonstrates respect and understanding towards the other person's viewpoint, even if it differs from your own. By attentively listening to the concerns and emotions of the other party, you can identify the root causes of the issue and address them more effectively.

Choosing the right timing and setting for the conversation is equally critical. Avoid discussing sensitive matters in public or in the midst of other distractions. Opt for a private and neutral location where both parties can feel comfortable and focused. Setting aside ample time for the conversation also allows for thorough discussion without feeling rushed.

When dealing with a difficult conversation, maintaining emotional control is essential. Remaining calm and composed, even in the face of disagreement or conflict, projects confidence and encourages a more constructive exchange. Avoid responding impulsively or defensively; instead, take a moment to gather your thoughts before articulating your perspective.

Additionally, using "I" statements can help express your feelings and concerns without appearing accusatory or confrontational. For instance, saying "I feel hurt when..." or "I am concerned about..." allows you to share your emotions without blaming or attacking the other person, facilitating a more open and non-defensive conversation. To foster a collaborative atmosphere, focus on finding solutions rather than dwelling on the problem itself.

Proposing alternative approaches or compromises demonstrates a willingness to work together to resolve the issue. Acknowledging any areas where you may have contributed to the problem can also create a more balanced and constructive conversation.

## STRATEGIES BUILDING CONFIDENCE IN SOCIAL GATHERINGS AND NETWORKING EVENTS

Building confidence in social gatherings and networking events is a valuable skill that can enhance personal and professional relationships and open doors to new opportunities. Here are some strategies to help individuals feel more self-assured and at ease in such settings:

Prepare and Set Goals: Before attending social gatherings or networking events, set clear and achievable goals for yourself. Define what you want to achieve during the event, such as meeting a specific number of new people, engaging in meaningful conversations, or sharing your interests and skills. Having clear objectives gives you a sense of purpose and direction, boosting your confidence as you approach the event.

Dress Confidently: Choose attire that makes you feel comfortable and confident. Dressing in a way that aligns with your personal style and makes you feel good about yourself can significantly impact your confidence levels. When you feel good in your appearance, it reflects in your body language and demeanor, positively influencing how others perceive you.

Practice Small Talk: Engaging in small talk is a common aspect of social gatherings and networking events. Practice simple conversation starters and be prepared to discuss common topics, such as current events, hobbies, or shared interests. Being well-prepared can help ease nervousness and initiate conversations more effortlessly.

Embrace Positive Body Language: Adopting positive body language can exude confidence and approachability. Maintain good posture, make eye contact, and offer warm smiles during interactions. Avoid crossing your arms or fidgeting, as these gestures can convey nervousness. Positive body language creates a welcoming presence and encourages others to approach you.

Focus on Listening: While networking, show genuine interest in the people you meet by actively listening to their stories and experiences. Being a good listener demonstrates respect and empathy, making others feel valued and appreciated. This attentiveness not only helps you build rapport but also allows you to gather valuable information about potential connections.

Overcome Rejection: Remember that not every interaction will lead to a deep connection or fruitful networking opportunity. Accept that rejection is a natural part of social interactions, and don't be disheartened by it. Building confidence involves embracing both positive and challenging experiences and learning from them.

Practice Mindfulness: Stay present and focus on the current moment rather than worrying about future interactions or outcomes. Practicing mindfulness helps you remain centered and calm, enabling you to make authentic connections and engage more meaningfully in conversations.

Celebrate Your Accomplishments: Acknowledge your achievements and strengths, both personally and professionally. Recognizing your capabilities and past successes can boost your self-confidence and give you a positive outlook in social settings.

# CHAPTER FIVE

## METHODS IN APPROACHING A STRANGER

Approaching strangers and initiating conversations is an essential skill for building new connections, whether in social settings or professional environments. Although it may seem daunting at first, mastering this skill can lead to enriching experiences and opportunities. The first step in approaching strangers is to adopt a positive and open demeanor. A warm smile and friendly body language create an approachable presence that encourages others to engage in conversation.

Starting with a simple greeting is a great way to break the ice. A genuine "Hello" or "Hi, how are you?" shows courtesy and sets a welcoming tone for the interaction. Finding common ground is key to keeping the conversation flowing. Observing the surroundings or the context in which you meet the person can provide cues for relevant discussion topics. Shared experiences or mutual interests serve as natural conversation starters, making it easier to connect with the other person.

As the conversation progresses, complimenting the individual or asking open-ended questions shows genuine interest in getting to know them better. Compliments can be about their outfit, work accomplishments, or any recent achievements. Asking questions about their hobbies, opinions, or experiences encourages them to share more about themselves, creating a deeper connection. Active listening is equally important during the conversation. Paying close attention to what the other person is saying and responding thoughtfully demonstrates respect and consideration for their thoughts and feelings.

It's important to be mindful of avoiding controversial topics, especially in the early stages of conversation. Stick to neutral subjects until you establish a more profound connection and better understanding of the person's preferences. Embracing rejection with a positive mindset is crucial. Not every individual may be receptive to initiating a conversation, and that's entirely normal. Taking rejection in stride and moving on to the next opportunity is part of the learning process.

## HANDLING SMALL TALK

Handling small talk and keeping conversations engaging are essential social skills that contribute to building meaningful connections and fostering enjoyable interactions. The key to successful small talk is being present and attentive. When engaging in small talk, focus on the person in front of you, actively listen to what they say, and show genuine interest in their thoughts and experiences. Being present allows you to respond thoughtfully and fosters a sense of connection, making the conversation more engaging for both participants.

Asking open-ended questions is a powerful technique to keep conversations flowing and engaging. These questions encourage the other person to provide more detailed responses, leading to deeper and more meaningful discussions. By avoiding yes-or-no inquiries and instead asking about their opinions, experiences, or interests, you create opportunities for the conversation to explore diverse topics and connect on a deeper level.

Additionally, sharing personal stories or experiences can contribute to more engaging conversations. Sharing something personal can create a sense of vulnerability and authenticity, which often encourages the other person to reciprocate and share their own stories. This mutual exchange of personal experiences deepens the connection and makes the conversation more memorable and enjoyable.

To maintain engagement, it's essential to find common interests and topics of mutual relevance. Discover shared hobbies, experiences, or passions that both participants can relate to. Discussing these shared interests naturally sparks enthusiasm and curiosity, leading to a more enjoyable and stimulating conversation.

## EFFECTIVE COMMUNICATION IN VIRTUAL ENVIRONMENTS

In today's digital age, effective communication in virtual environments is more crucial than ever. Communicating with confidence in virtual and digital settings is essential for making a strong impact, building relationships, and achieving success in both personal and professional realms. To exude confidence in virtual interactions, preparation is key. Before engaging in video calls, webinars, or virtual meetings, take the time to organize your thoughts and key points. Having a clear structure for your message will help you deliver it with conviction and clarity, ensuring that your audience understands and retains the information.

Maintaining positive body language during virtual communication is equally important. In video calls, maintain eye contact by looking into the camera when speaking, as it gives the impression of direct engagement with your audience. Sit or stand upright, and avoid distracting gestures to project confidence and professionalism. Additionally, use gestures and facial expressions effectively to enhance your message and keep your audience engaged.

In digital written communication, such as emails or instant messaging, choose your words carefully to ensure a confident tone. Be concise and clear in your messages, getting to the point quickly to respect your recipients' time and attention. Avoid using excessive exclamation points or all caps, as they can come across as aggressive. Instead, use positive language and tailor your communication to the recipient's preferences and context, which demonstrates adaptability and consideration.

To enhance your confidence in virtual environments, practice active listening. Pay close attention to what others are saying during video conferences or virtual meetings, and respond thoughtfully. Demonstrating that you are fully engaged in the conversation not only builds rapport but also helps you articulate your thoughts more confidently when it's your turn to speak. Additionally, be open to constructive feedback, as it provides opportunities for growth and improvement in your communication skills.

## DEALING WITH CONFLICT AND DIFFICULT INDIVIDUALS

Dealing with conflict and difficult individuals is a challenging yet essential aspect of personal and professional life. Conflict can arise from differences in opinions, goals, or personalities, leading to tense situations. When faced with conflict, it's crucial to remain calm and composed. Take a step back and assess the situation objectively to understand the root cause of the conflict. Listen actively to the other person's perspective and avoid jumping to conclusions. By showing empathy and understanding, you can lay the groundwork for resolving the conflict amicably.

Addressing conflict and difficult individuals requires effective communication. Choose your words carefully and avoid confrontational language that could escalate the situation. Focus on expressing your concerns and needs in a clear and assertive manner. At the same time, be receptive to feedback and be open to finding a compromise or solution that works for both parties. Encourage the other person to do the same, creating a constructive environment for resolving the conflict.

It's essential to maintain respect for the other person's viewpoint, even if you disagree. Avoid personal attacks or blame, as they can intensify the conflict and damage relationships. Instead, focus on the issue at hand and brainstorm potential solutions together. Showing respect and empathy toward the other person's feelings and perspectives can foster a more cooperative atmosphere and lead to a more satisfactory resolution.

In dealing with difficult individuals, practice patience and self-control. Difficult people may exhibit challenging behaviors, such as aggression, negativity, or defensiveness. Stay composed and refrain from reacting emotionally. Seek to understand their motivations or underlying concerns, and acknowledge their emotions without necessarily accepting their behavior. Setting boundaries and maintaining a calm demeanor can help diffuse tense situations and facilitate more productive interactions.

## RESOLVING MISUNDERSTANDINGS

Resolving misunderstandings is crucial for building stronger connections in both personal and professional relationships. Misunderstandings can arise from miscommunication, differing perspectives, or assumptions. To address and overcome misunderstandings, open and honest communication is essential. Approach the other person with a willingness to understand their viewpoint and clarify your own. Actively listen to their concerns and acknowledge their feelings, demonstrating empathy and respect.

In resolving misunderstandings, refrain from placing blame or making assumptions about the other person's intentions. Instead, focus on the specific issue at hand and avoid bringing up past grievances. Remain objective and seek to find common ground or shared understanding. By addressing the root cause of the misunderstanding, you can work towards a more meaningful resolution that strengthens the connection.

In some cases, misunderstandings may result from cultural or language differences. When communicating with individuals from diverse backgrounds, be aware of potential cultural nuances and adapt your communication style accordingly. Be patient and understanding, and be willing to clarify and explain your perspective to bridge any cultural gaps.

Building stronger connections after resolving misunderstandings requires ongoing efforts. Cultivate open communication, and create a safe space where both parties feel comfortable sharing their thoughts and feelings. Foster mutual trust and respect by being reliable and following through on commitments. Show appreciation for the other person's efforts and contributions, which can reinforce the connection and build a positive rapport.

Lastly, be mindful of your non-verbal communication, as it can impact the strength of your connection. Maintain positive body language, such as making eye contact and offering genuine smiles, to convey warmth and approachability. A friendly and supportive demeanor can enhance the connection and create a more conducive environment for open and honest communication.

# CONCLUSION

"Conquer Your Communication: A Step-by-Step Guide to Confidence in Conversations" is an empowering resource that equips individuals with the tools and strategies needed to master the art of effective communication. Throughout this comprehensive guide, readers have learned how to exude confidence, engage with diverse personalities, and navigate various communication platforms with ease.

With this invaluable guide in hand, individuals can now approach any conversation, whether virtual or in-person, with the utmost self-assurance. They have discovered the power of active listening, empathy, and adaptability in fostering meaningful connections with others. By tailoring their communication to diverse personalities and situations, readers have unlocked the key to successful interpersonal relationships.

"Conquer Your Communication" has emphasized the significance of body language, powerful vocabulary, and persuasive language to leave a lasting impact in any interaction. Furthermore, this guide has provided invaluable insights into handling conflicts, resolving misunderstandings, and building stronger connections that stand the test of time.

Armed with the knowledge and practical tips shared in this guide, readers are now poised to conquer any communication challenge and seize opportunities that await them. They are well-equipped to thrive both professionally and personally, transforming their interactions into memorable and impactful experiences.

As individuals embrace the principles within this guide, they will witness a profound transformation in their communication skills and, in turn, see their confidence soar to new heights. With "Conquer Your Communication" as their steadfast companion, readers can navigate the complexities of communication with grace and assertiveness, leaving a trail of meaningful connections and accomplishments in their wake. Embark on this journey to master the art of confident communication and unlock the boundless potential that awaits us all.

www.ingramcontent.com/pod-product-compliance
Lightning Source LLC
Chambersburg PA
CBHW062247290526
45794CB00006B/2450